T0157886

The Alphabet of Success

The Alphabet of Success:

"Let the life you want become the life you live!"

Jai A. Ingraham, MPA

"The Inspirational Motivator"

authorHOUSE®

AuthorHouse™
1663 Liberty Drive
Bloomington, IN 47403
www.authorhouse.com
Phone: 1-800-839-8640

Published by AuthorHouse   05/03/2012

ISBN: 978-1-4685-8126-3 (sc)
ISBN: 978-1-4685-8127-0 (e)

Contents

Dedication

This book is dedicated to the memory of my grandmother Atheria Glass Ingraham. Her wisdom still guides me and her love continues to give me strength. Even though she lived for 83 years, I still say she's gone too soon! As I completed this work, I could hear her poignant words so clearly, "So be it and God bless it." Thanks Thera!

Acknowledgements

First of all, I must give thanks to my Heavenly Father who is the giver of every good and perfect gift. It is truly *All Because of Jesus (*thanks Andrae Crouch), that I am here. I realize that my life is a miracle. I cherish everyday as a gift. I want to thank Him for how He has immensely kept and favored me. He has given me the vision and the words to say. All I ever want to do is His will!!!

I also want to thank my family. To my wife Karen, not only are you a source of inspiration but you are also my greatest encourager and my best critic. I am because we are. To my daughters Kiara and Jaicey, thank you for being the best part of me rising every day and the best reason to come home. To my mother, Sonja, thank you for making the decision to have me. You have taught me how to endure all things with dignity. To my brothers Jon and AnTony you are both faithful and priceless. To my sister Jenein, you are one of a kind. To my father the Late Joseph A. Ingraham, thank you for equipping me with the tools to be the man I have become. To the rest of my family (and extended family) I love you all!!!

Along the way there have been a number of persons that have poured into my development as a "messenger" of hope to world. As a Christian, educator, speaker, singer, trainer and author I have crossed many kindred spirits.

I want to thank Poet and Author Avis P. Raines for being a mentor, friend, colleague and supporter. Her insight and help in the writing process through the years (especially on this project) has been invaluable. I also want to sincerely thank her for lending her masterful words in the Forward. We met several years ago and have built a formidable bond. I am proud to have her on my team!

I also want to thank my brother Jon for serving as my first "unofficial" editor. You are wise beyond your years. Special thanks also goes to Aluysius Noble a fine educator and professional in his own right for lending his expertise to this work.

To my entire African Methodist Episcopal Church Family (specifically St. Paul A.M.E. Church, Miami, Florida; the Eleventh Episcopal District and the Lay Organization at all levels) thank you for your spiritual nourishment, love and support. A very special thanks goes to Rev. Robert Jackson, III, and Rev. Melvin Payne, Jr. for always having *"faith in your friend."* Most especially, I want to thank the Most Noble Dr. Edward J. Braynon, Jr. 30th Grand Basileus, The Omega Psi Phi Fraternity, Inc. for his words of affirmation. From him I have learned that, *"Friendship Is Essential to the Soul."*

To my other families: Clark Atlanta University, Florida International University, St. Thomas University, Northeastern University, Omega Psi Phi Fraternity (Sigma Alpha Chapter), Prince Hall Masonry (New Providence Lodge #365, Miami, Florida), Kazah Temple #149, A.E.A.O.N.M.S., Fatherhood Task Force of South Florida, University of Phoenix, The School Board of Broward County and Miami-Dade County Public Schools you all have had an integral role in the development of my message.

Lastly, I want to thank you for reading this book. My development as a messenger of hope is forever evolving. It is my prayer that something said in this book touches you in a way that your life will be forever changed. Your investment in me has already changed my life forever!

Forward
By Acclaimed Poet and Author Avis P. Raines

The Alphabet of Success is a powerful, must have self-help book that puts you on the right path for greatness. I think that a lot of us set ourselves up for failure without even realizing it, due to lack of preparation. Most of us just dive right in without even analyzing things or giving it a second thought. Well, let me tell you, if it's preparation you need, then it's preparation you will get. Jai has taken his wealth of knowledge as an educator, speaker and motivator to create a jewel of inspiration in this work.

The Alphabet of Success will provide you with various techniques and strategies needed to make sure that all your steps are in order prior to venturing out, or treading new waters. You will be empowered with all the necessary instruments to successfully conquer your goals. It even assists you with existing situations you may face.

The Alphabet of Success gives intuitive perspectives on life by examining failed attempts or yet-to-be conquered dreams. By acknowledging these factors, Jai will help you to strengthen various aspects of your life. This book will encourage you to try again and find different approaches to accomplishing your goals. Whether it's a word of advice or encouragement in spoken or written form, we all need the driving force of motivation. Trust me when I say that *The Alphabet of Success* is encouraging, enlightening, insightful, but most of all deeply inspirational. So, if you don't mind tapping into a new you, a better you; then this is just the book you need. Believe me when I say it's definitely worth a gander from cover to cover. So read, learn, and enjoy!

Introduction

The mind and the ability to reason, quite possibly are the greatest gifts that God gave to human beings. In His Divine wisdom He left it up to each individual to decide how they choose to facilitate the course of their life. We have the right to choose between what is right and what is wrong. More importantly, we have the right to choose to move forward in a positive manner or digress in a state of perpetual indecisiveness.

Just as the mind is a powerful tool, the dilemma of choice provides an ongoing inward struggle between knowing what can be done and doing what must be done. Every experience in life has its own value. At any particular moment you may deem an experience to be positive or negative, but it is always relative.

After working for close to 20 years, I have observed that the one thing that all people have in common is emotion. How you feel about yourself and relate to others denotes how you will handle every situation that may arise in your life. Your reaction to circumstances can determine your level of success or your rate of failure.

I felt compelled to write this book as a testament to the very best that lies within all of us. Every person that has ever walked the face the earth has a set of pre-designated tools which entitles them to be successful. Unfortunately for many, this much sought after "success" lies dormant because they can never see past the state of where they are. It is my prayer that *The Alphabet of Success* will help you to, "Let the life you want, become the life you live!"

Yours in Life,

Jai A. Ingraham, MPA
"The Inspirational Motivator"

"A"

Anger Leads to Atonement

"All misfortune is but a stepping stone to fortune."
—Henry David Thoreau

Pissed off! Mad as hell! Livid! Upset! Enraged! Outraged! (And my personal favorite) Thirty-Eight Hot! Any of these expressions ring a bell? They all describe one thing . . . ANGER! If you say that you've never felt that way about anything, you are lying to the world as well as yourself.

Anger is a basic human emotion that comes as an inward reaction to something that has happened outwardly in a negative fashion. Usually someone has done or said something to upset you. Or perhaps you may have experienced a tragic sense of loss. Nevertheless, anger becomes a source of pain.

Anger can also be both positive and negative. It would be considered negative with regards to an abrupt reaction to an event or circumstance. Misfortune is a necessary part of life. However, anger should be considered positive when it leads to a sense of motivation and enlightenment. The process of enlightenment can lead to an awakening of Atonement.

Atonement comes when you are able to reflect upon all the experiences that you have had and take account of them. Atonement is nothing more than the acknowledgement of your actions. A major part of this process is taking ownership of your responsibility to grow.

Throughout my life, I often think of decisions that I have made as a result of anger. Whether it was being impatient with a fellow employee, addressing the needs of a wayward student, or letting pride take precedence over patience, my inner-voice would always tell me that there was a better way. Atonement gives you a chance to put the broken pieces back together again.

Yes, your growth (or a lack thereof) is based upon decisions you make. In this period of time you will be able to make peace with yourself and move forward in your life with complete confidence. Search within yourself to identify target areas for self-improvement. You are always worth the investment!

"B"

Once Belittled . . . Twice a Believer . . . Now a Becomer!

*"The direction of our life's journey begins to become
clear when we claim our own shortcomings."*
—Dr. Bettye J. Allen

Whether we want to believe it or not, there is a little inferiority complex in all of us. Some of the people that have reached heights of greatness in their respective fields; i.e. Michael Jordan, Donald Trump, Chuck Norris, Sean "P. Diddy" Combs and even President Barack H. Obama all at some point dealt with feelings of personal inadequacy.

Peer pressure is real and more importantly it is powerful. The emotional and psychological scars that come being the victim of being belittled can rock a person to the core. Statistics show that there has been a significant rise in bullying across all aspects of society. Additionally, what is also most disheartening is when feelings of belittlement and despair are self-imposed. Nothing is worse than when a person plants seeds of weeds in their own garden of achievement.

Fortunately, the remedy for feelings of inadequacy and belittlement is the power of positive belief; more specifically, belief in the power of self. There is greatness in all of us. You already have everything that you need to become everything that you want! (That last statement was powerful! You may want to read it again!!!) ☺

Sometimes you may be on the brink of a breakthrough but you are blinded by your own lack of belief. While in my senior year of undergraduate studies at Clark Atlanta University, Professor of Political Science and Department Chair, the late Dr. Michael S. Bailey said to me, "Son you can only be a great as you mind will allow you to be!" Still trying to "find" myself back then, those words were a beacon of light to me. They are even more meaningful in my life today.

Once you have mastered the power of positive belief, you can move into the land of "Becoming". When you are a "Becomer" you are able to break the shackles of low self-esteem, pessimism and low-living. Because you were "Belittled", you now "Believe" in your ability to be a "Becomer". Go get the job done!

"C"

Consequences Lead to Change

*"The world hates change, yet it is the only
thing that has brought progress."*
—Charles F. Kettering

The power of choice is immeasurable. Sir Isaac Newton's
Third Law of Motion states, "For every action there is an equal
and opposite reaction." Therefore, for everything that you do,
there is a price to pay. There will always a force pulling in the
opposite direction of where you are trying to go.

As we travel through life, we must be willing to face the reality
that exists. However, facing your reality does not necessarily
mean that you have to accept it. In order to improve your
state, you must recognize your ability to improve the situation
and yourself.

Positive change will only happen when you become passionate
and totally dissatisfied about the state of where you are. You
have got to want to change the state of your mind in order to
redirect the energy that is around you. Each one of us has
the power to positively or negatively impact our environment.

You must daily regiment your thoughts and actions around the question, "How bad do I want it?" If you want something bad enough, you will take the necessary steps to make reality appear.

I learned this lesson first hand with a serious health scare. On Wednesday, August 27, 2008 at the ripe old age of 30, I saw my life flash before my eyes. While sitting at my desk at work my heart began to race, I began to sweat, and I could not catch my breath. I drank a bottle of water thinking that would immediately help the situation. Seeing no relief, I casually told my co-worker, "Hey man, I'm not feeling too well, I think you better call 9-1-1." He looked at me in disbelief and placed the call. Waiting for the paramedics to come, all I can remember thinking is, "Man, I am too young to go out like this! Who is going to care for my wife and daughters?" Needless to say, I was scared. The paramedics finally arrived. They checked me out, and offered to take me out on a stretcher. I WOULD NOT LET THEM!!! I do not think I would have been able to live that experience down. However, my wife did later take me to the hospital. After a battery of exams, blood work and some much needed time off from work, it was determined that I did not have a heart attack but a heightened level of stress. They call it the "silent killer".

This unfortunate scenario made me deal with the consequences of not taking care of myself. These consequences forced me to make some serious lifestyle changes. I went from weighing 255 pounds to a trim 200 pounds. I began to exercise regularly and seriously manage my diet. I later found that this would become a key ingredient in maintaining positive energy for my life.

As you deal with challenges, know that the end result of the situation will be determined based upon how you deal with the consequences. Remember, change is always the only constant. Be your own change agent!

"D"

Discomfort Leads to Disruption

"Character may be manifested in the great moments, but it is made in the small ones."
—Phillips Brooks

As a child, I can remember the joy of shaking up a two liter bottle of soda to watch it explode when someone else tried to open it. The pressure that built up inside created a kinetic burst of energy that had to be released.

Pain in our lives functions in much the same manner as the soda in the bottle. Sometimes pain will make us feel so much discomfort that it becomes unbearable.

In thinking of pain, I cannot help but think of the story of Tyler Perry. The world now knows Tyler Perry as a great producer, director, actor, playwright and philanthropist. However, in telling his story Tyler often mentions that he came from a place of discomfort and despair before achieving success. Having been homeless and the subject of sexual abuse of as child, he has had to summon the will to demand greatness from within.

He came from a place of despair with determination to claim his destiny.

The positive antidote for this surprisingly lies within the action of disruption. A disruption can lead to an emotional, spiritual, physical and even financial "awakening" in your life. There is no way to get to the point of disruption without going through the process of discomfort. Every feeling and experience has value. Always embrace the journey!

"E"

Move from Excuses to Excellence!

"Discipline yourself to be obedient."
—Pastor Laura Pickett

"The time isn't right!" "It just isn't meant to be." "I'll do it tomorrow." "I'll get to it later!" "It's too hard!" "They already know who they are going to hire." "I'm too late." "She'll never notice me!" "I don't have a degree!" "He won't take my call." "There is too much paperwork to complete." (And my all-time favorite) "I just can't do it!"

The previous list was full of commonly used excuses. I must admit that I have used several of them in the past as explanations for not achieving. Some would define excuses as reasons for failure. The *American Heritage Dictionary* defines it as: 1) to offer an apology or explanation for (a fault or offense); 2) to justify; 3) to free as from an obligation. These definitions work well, but I would define an excuse as a personal sabotage on a prophetic promise!

11

One of my favorite historical figures is Chaka Zulu. The story of Chaka Zulu was made famous in the 1987 television mini-series *Chaka Zulu*. Chaka Zulu was a fierce 18th century African King and warrior. Chaka born out of wedlock was an outcast as a child and had to fight his way to the throne. His execution as a warrior was extraordinary. Chaka never made excuses for his circumstance. He used his plight as a means to fuel conquest for power. Although his thirst for power is what eventually led to an early death at the approximate age of 41, his self-reliance and discipline are admirable.

Execution is the declaration of accepted greatness. Obedience to the discipline of self is an important aspect of being successful. This will lead you to the excellence you seek. It is something as simple as making a decision to make that phone call, or to send that email, or to finish that job application. The most powerful opportunity is your next one! Decide to make that move, today!

"F"

Faith Leads to Freedom

*"Without faithfulness, the sum total of
your other great talents is diluted."*
—Rev. Dr. James Merrit

Have you ever been so bogged down that you did not feel like you were going to make it? I know I have. Life tends just to be that way. Whether it's finances, college exams, a difficult spouse, health issues, or just feelings of being overwhelmed, life can sometimes make you question your very existence.

Finding strength in your faith is how you will reach your breakthrough. Looking at life from a human perspective will only limit your vision. However, depending on or trusting your faith can give you peace in the middle of a storm.

For some faith seems as a larger than life concept that can only be attributed to miraculous events or manifestation of great Divine Intervention. However, faith can be something as simple as consistently rising out of bed in the morning and making a decision to plant your feet on the ground and walk. That's faith. Perhaps even taking the chance of sitting in an upright chair without inspecting it first, could be considered an act of faith. Whether it is great or small, belief coupled with action, leads to faith.

For every obstacle you face, there is a measure of faith to get you to your own "promised land". 2 Timothy 2:13 (NASB) states, "If we are faithless, He remains faithful, for He cannot deny Himself." The freedom that comes from knowing that you have reached inner peace is immeasurable. When it comes to your faith, the limits that exist are the ones you put on yourself. Freedom is your currency for success. Don't spend it all in one place!

"G"

Got Success?

"To know what you prefer instead of humbly saying 'Amen' to what the world tells you you ought to prefer, is to have kept your soul alive."
—Robert Louis Stevenson

One of the greatest marketing slogans I remember from the 1980's was, "It's in there!" This slogan was made famous by the spaghetti sauce brand Prego. Although it wasn't homemade, many would agree that it was the next best thing.

Well, I think that Prego did get it right. Every one of us has some really interesting things inside of us. These things are simple and complex, negative and positive, or public and private. Nevertheless, it is indeed all in there. Never allow other's opinions about you to take precedence over your own intuition for your life.

We should not try to deny what is inside. You cannot deny who and what you are. There may be some things about yourself that you may like or want to improve or even change. That is fine. However, you owe it to yourself to embrace ALL the possibilities of what you can become.

There is only one sure way to accomplish your mission of being successful. Boldly declare that you will always demand the very best from yourself! Success isn't magic; it's simply mastering your WILL over a lifetime. It is a never-ending process of discovery. There is an ancient Chinese proverb which says, "Haste does not bring success." I truly believe in the title of DeBarge's 1983 classic song, *Time Will Reveal.*

"H"

Hatred Leads to Healing

"The true measure of a man is how he treats someone who can absolutely do him no good."
—Samuel Johnson

Although I was not alive during the American Civil Rights Movement, I am well aware of the sacrifices made by many people (of all races, creeds and backgrounds) regarding racial equality and the need for social change.

I remember in 1988 when the movie *Mississippi Burning* was released in movie theaters. As a young child, I was terrified by the sight of a man being taken out of his home, beaten in front of his family, home burned to the ground, and then lynched by racists in the backyard of his own property! Now if that isn't a just reason to warrant feelings of hatred towards the oppressors, I don't know what is!!!

In order for a person to move from being a "victim" to a "victor", they must look past their place of hurt and focus on the promise of forgiveness. The key is not to forget what was done but to release the negative energy that festers within as a result of what has happened in the past. When this happens, hatred can give way to healing for the heart, mind and spirit. Think about what the power of forgiveness has done for you in your life. It is a gift that is always worth the price!

"I"

Ignorance Fuels Regret

*Good judgment comes from experience, and
a lot of that comes from bad judgment.*
—Will Rogers

There is a well-known saying which states, "If I had only known then what I know now." If I had a dollar for every time I heard that expression, I would be a very rich man. If I had five dollars for every time that I've used that expression myself, I'd be a booming tycoon! ☺

Many people make mistakes in life because they simply don't know any better. Ignorance should never be an excuse for not reaching your full potential. If there is something that you don't know, learn more about it. There is always someone that has traveled down the road that you are about to travel.

One of the many joys in my life is being able to give guidance and advice to others. Sometimes people just need to know that there are others who can relate to their experience. Primarily, young people and adults going through transitions find themselves asking the questions: Why? How? & When? I recognize that a great deal of my successful has come because I've saturated my life with people who know more than I do and are willing to share. Knowledge is most potent when it is given away.

The worst feeling ever is to know that you have missed an opportunity because you were misinformed or worse, uninformed. It is one thing to get bad information but it's another not to have gotten any information at all. So, from now on instead of saying "I wish", say "I will." Then you will proudly be able to say, "I'm glad I did!"

"J"

Jealousy is Dangerous!

"The jealous know nothing, suspect much and fear everything."
—Curt Goetz

Have you ever seen someone with something you wanted and been in awe of them? It may have been a job, car, financial increase or even a new relationship. Well, I truly believe that provisions have already been made for every person to be the very best that they can. Every person must be willing to embrace it. Noted Author and Minister, Laura Pickett, in her book ***It's Time to Bring Forth*** states, *". . . there comes a time after much confessing, much sowing and much believing, for you to see what you've been waiting for!"* If you are able to focus on what already belongs to you, then you will be able to receive the "extra" that is to come.

There is no need to be envious of other people. Jealousy can produce feelings of hatred, greed, deceit and unfaithfulness. These negative feelings come as a result of not being comfortable with where you are and not being appreciative of what you have. The gifts and talents that you possess are more than enough to meet all of your wants and needs.

Success demands that you embrace your own humanity. Don't run from it. Acknowledge your humanity. Use the gifts that you have, whatever they may be. So, instead of being jealous of others, ask God to direct your path to unlock the best that comes from within!

"K"

Know How to Make Your Own Opportunity

"Indecision is the greatest thief of opportunity."
—Jim Rohn

You have been searching for your breakthrough and you have been waiting for your ship to arrive. Have you ever asked yourself the following questions: When is my time going to come? Why can't I get ahead? Or, when is it going to be my time to shine?

Well, there is a wise saying which states, "Be the opportunity that you are waiting for!" Never allow fear to keep you from reaching your full potential!" So many times people sell themselves short because they were unwilling to step out on faith. There comes a time when you must be willing to "go out into the deep."

Some of the best people in their respective fields only got there because they made an opportunity. Chance becomes opportunity when initiative meets determination. If there is something that you want to accomplish, be dogmatically driven in your quest. There is nothing wrong with hard work or failure. They are both key landmarks of the road of success. Remember, no one said that the road would be easy. That's why most perilous journeys arc traveled alone. However, determination and faith in yourself will help to guide you along the way. You can make it!

"L"

Living, Loving and Lifting . . .

"Those who loved you and were helped
by you will remember you. So carve your
name on hearts and not on marble."
—C. H. Spurgeon

The most important aspect of human existence is the ability to live. Now, I know that this concept may seem self-explanatory, but I don't think this notion should be taken lightly. Life is truly a gift, and it should be celebrated.

Every person has a responsibility to give the best of themselves to all they encounter. Life void of love is lunacy. I would not want to live life without love. Love is the currency of universal language. All types of love are important: love for humanity, friends, family, strangers, enemies, (yes I did say enemies), and most importantly, love for self. Self-love makes all other forms of love possible.

Lifting involves making the time to invest in others. If you want to be successful you must help others reach their full potential. An out-stretched hand can be the difference between someone reaching their destiny or losing all hope. Never underestimate the power of human interaction. Your touch is powerful!

"M"
Move Beyond
What You Can See!

"Everyone who has ever taken a shower has had an idea. It's the person who gets out of the shower, dries off, and does something about it that makes a difference."
—Nolan Bushnell

Living in South Florida, I can attest to the fact that we have some of the most beautiful beaches in the world. As a child, I would often go to the beach with my parents just to be able to put my feet in the sand. I often wondered how ships would be able to navigate the waters of the high seas. Even as an adult, I love to go to the beach and walk along the shore line.

In looking at the awesome vastness of the ocean, there is a point where you are unable to tell its beginning from its ending. We now know that on the other side of the ocean, there are other nations and people with various cultures and beliefs. However, it took courageous explorers to change the theory that the world was flat. Today, that idea sounds absurd.

But then, so does the idea of paying almost $5.00 for a gallon of gas!

Any great accomplishment begins with a simple belief that it can be done. This new found belief can be derailed before it reaches its final destination because a lack of what I like to call "wide-lens" vision. Most people only use "single-lens" vision because that is their immediate point of reference. As human beings we want to do what is most comfortable and convenient. However, using "wide-lens" vision will help you to navigate the rough seas or (storms) that may come in your life. Simultaneously, this will help prepare you to handle success when it comes your way. Trust me, if you are diligent and faithful it will come. You may not see it now, but it's out there!

"N"

Nothing to Lose & Everything to Gain!

"Ordinary riches can be stolen, real riches cannot. In your soul are infinitely precious things that cannot be taken from you."
—Oscar Wilde

Every day as I drive around town, I see scores of what I assume to be homeless people on the streets. However, I think the more applicable term to use would be "displaced". As I see these persons, I often ask the question, "What happened in that person's life in order for them to be where they are." Well, curiosity led me to do a little digging.

Next to one of my favorite local book stores, I met a displaced gentleman. For the purpose of this story we will call him "Jim". When I was exiting the book store, Jim asked me if I had any spare change. Instead of giving him money, I asked him if he would mind telling me his story. He was shocked. Jim was somewhat taken aback because no one had ever asked him to tell his story. Jim went on to state that back during 1992 he lost everything he had as a result of Hurricane Andrew. He said that he just had not been able to get back on his feet and he lost touch with his family. After listening to his story, I gave him some cash and said a prayer with him. I never saw Jim again.

Jim's story has stayed with me. His story was a wake-up call for me to acknowledge those areas in my own life where I have been "displaced". If we are all honest, in some way we have all been displaced.

The only certainty in life is the uncertainty of its nature. If you are not grounded at your core in faith, then you won't have anything to draw from when life throws you a series of curve balls. At any given moment the world may be yours to lose or gain. In order to be successful, don't fear being displaced. Decide now to find triumph even in the midst of tragedy!

"O"

Oppression Leads to Overcoming

"Please take responsibility for the energy you bring into this place."
—Dr. Jill Taylor

Have you ever been so disenchanted that you can't see how you are going to move forward? The state of where you are sometimes has an overwhelming influence on how you see yourself. It also can have an impact on how, when and why others interact with you.

When you are oppressed, you feel the pressure of the world pressing down on you. In order to deal with this feeling, you must be willing to embrace your discomfort in order to embark on your journey.

Surprisingly, there are fruits of knowledge from feeling oppressed. If all of your experiences are positive, uplifting and enjoyable, how then can you truly know what it means to grow, evolve or become? Having an overcoming spirit means invoking a great understanding of what it means to endure, engage and adapt to every situation. Positive energy is contagious. It is important to give and receive it.

In order to truly overcome, we must truly submit to the best that is within ourselves. Just be open to the possibility of what the future may hold. I think Oprah Winfrey says it best, "Start embracing the life that is calling you and use your life to serve the world!" We all have the ability. Make up your mind that you are going to use it!

"P"

Passion Reigns Supreme

"Passion is the genesis of genius."
—Anthony Robbins

There is a popular saying that "variety is the spice of life." If this is true then this premise is good for the heart, mind and spirit. As human beings, we are innately spiritual creatures that sometimes put too much emphasis on the physical realm of our existence. There must be balance in order to significantly impact the fullness of the lives that we live.

Ultimately, you must make a decision that you are going to chose to put yourself first. Now, I know that on the surface this may seem like an arrogant, pompous and self-serving ideology to practice. However, I do mean it in the best possible way. It is impossible to do anything positive if you don't have a clear understanding of what makes you tick. Often times, we try to do everything for others without taking time to do what is important for ourselves.

There should be no one aspect of your life that totally dominates or takes precedence over the other. There is nothing wrong with having a career. But, if that career is the basis for how you define yourself or is the only validation of worth that you have in your life, I would say that it is time to make some adjustments.

Contrary to popular belief, it is ok to really ENJOY your life. You have an obligation to live or "play" throughout your life with passion. Passion is the driving energy of force that will help you accomplish everything that will be great in your life. Passion is what will drive you to keep going when your body is past tired, your finances are on life support, your family just does not understand and your spirit has been "tried by the fire." If you are going to do it, you should love it! Otherwise, it is just a waste of time. Your time and passion are much too valuable for that!

"Q"

Questions Lead to Quality

*"The key to wisdom is asking
all the right questions."*
—John A. Simone, Sr.

My Pastor, Rev. Robert Jackson, III often says, "It is ok to question God!" I have to say that the first time I heard this is I was a little skeptical of it. However, as a child in elementary school I was taught that the only stupid question is the one that you don't ask. So, there is something to be said for going directly to the source when there is information you seek. One of my favorite passages of scripture is, "We have not because we ask not." (James 4:2.)

Asking the right question, at the right time, to the right person can be the difference between you experiencing greatness or wasting away in a pool of mediocrity. There is no one person walking the face of the Earth that can claim to have all of the information that is needed to be successful. All of us live by the experience of trial and error. However, due to the vast experiences that we all have, valuable tangible research on

35

life's "best practices" has been already been published. Your chapter has yet to be written.

The quality of your life of your life can be significantly improved based upon the questions that you are willing to ask. Whether you are searching for career advice, spiritual guidance, personal clarity, financial stability or physical wellness there are answers to the questions you seek. Your thirst for knowledge should never be quenched. Pride is the "evil step mother" of wisdom. You will never know what you can accomplish if you are too proud to admit what you don't know. So, ask the questions that you need to and get the information you need to grow your own success. Remember, a life of quality is your destiny!

"R"

Rejection Leads to Resurrection

"Perseverance is failing nineteen times
and succeeding the twentieth."
—Julie Andrews

There is an old shoe box full of old letters that I keep at my mother's house. They are professional rejection letters. (All of the old love letters have been destroyed . . .)☺ Yes, I am proud to say that I have been rejected from some of the greatest professionally entities in the world. Once upon a time I had a fervent interest in law enforcement. I went on interviews and submitted applications for various local, state and federal agencies.

There is one particular story of rejection that I am extremely proud of. In 2001, I submitted and application to become a Special Agent with the Drug Enforcement Administration (DEA). Yes, I did say DEA. I went through the entire process. I filled out the all of the paperwork, passed the written exam, and survived the panel interview. However, on two separate occasions I did not pass the Physical Agility Test (PAT). Now, it has been some 10 years, but the test was the most strenuous of all the federal law enforcement agencies. The test included, wind sprints, pull-ups, push-ups, sit-ups, a firearm trigger pull exercise, and it culminated with a two mile run. All of these exercises were timed and completed concurrently.

Now to be truthfully honest, I never considered myself to be much of an athlete. So prior to the first PAT I did not put forth maximum effort in training. It showed. When it came time for me to complete the 2 mile run I did not make it past the 3rd lap around the track. So, several months later on my second attempt at the PAT I doubled my score in every category of the test. There were three of us completing the 2 mile run together. For the first 6 laps, I kept pace with the rest of the pack. However, on the final 2 laps I was unable to keep pace with the other runners. Needless to say I completed the run with a respectable time, but it was not the time necessary to continue in the application process.

Although I never became a DEA Agent, I was extremely proud of the fact that I went through the process. All of the law enforcement agencies had their reasons for rejecting me. It was not because I had done anything wrong or because I was not qualified. It just was not what I was supposed to be doing. Sometimes when a person goes through a lot of rejection, they reach a point when they begin to feel really bad about themselves. They lose sight of the power of possibility . . .

Ultimately, the rejection of not having a career in law enforcement led to a personal, professional and spiritual resurrection in my life. Personally, I made a decision to focus on investing in my relationship (marriage). Professionally, I discovered that my true calling was serving others through the vehicle of education. Spiritually, God showed me the importance of listening to His voice and not following my own path. Success is best served with Divine Intervention!

"S"

Service is a Way of Life

*"Based on the gift they have received,
everyone should use it to serve others, as good
managers of the varied grace of God."*
—1Peter 4:10; (version unknown)

I believe Dr. Martin Luther King, Jr. said it best, "Everyone can be great because everyone can serve." These poignant words have been heard by many over the years but I wonder if they are actually internalized. Service is just like respect, in order to receive it you have got to be willing to give it, freely.

However, service should not be treated like your favorite winter coat or pair of jeans. It can't be something that you try or only do as a hobby. In order for it to be effective or meaningful, it MUST become a way of life. Success demands that you give the very best of yourself to others. Look for ways to focus and harness your own positive energy to make others discover their own.

Service to others is also important because it helps to perpetuate an ongoing cycle of gregarious engagement. Some would argue that authentic communication is a dying art form. There is tremendous power in connecting with others. The human spirit feeds on tangible connectivity. This is why newborn infants need the body heat of their mothers in order to survive. You should never underestimate your power and responsibility to positively impact others. Remember, you never know when you may be in need of the same "service" that you render to others. There are benefits to giving others your best. It comes back to you!

"𝔗"

𝔗ragedy Can 𝔏ead to 𝔗riumph

> *"Tragedy is a tool for the living to gain*
> *wisdom, not a guide by which to live."*
> —Robert Francis Kennedy

When history chronicles the accomplishments of great American Presidents I'm not sure where it would chronicle President George W. Bush. In retrospect, I can honestly say that I do have a fond memory of an event that happened during his tenure. Unfortunately, it was at one of the worst times in my life and in the life of our country.

On, September 10, 2001, my father (and also the greatest man I've ever known) Joseph Antonio Ingraham passed away on my 24th birthday at home with me. It was a Monday. He was 49 years old.

The next morning, I can remember sleeping in the bed with my mom because she did not want to sleep alone. That Tuesday morning, September 11th I recall turning on the television and seeing one of the "Twin Towers" of the World Trade Center on fire. A short while later I saw a plane hit the second tower. We were under attack . . .

Now in the midst of my personal tragedy and in our nation's devastating tragedy, I actually found comfort in the immediate, swift action taken by President Bush. In that moment he gave the best of himself. He stood tall in our darkest hour because the nation needed him to.

Although the loss of my father hurt tremendously, it paled in comparison to the magnitude of what happened on September 11th. I realized how blessed I was. My father died in the peace of his own home, sitting on the sofa, with me on my birthday. What a gift! Families of those that tragically lost their lives the very next day were not as fortunate. Many of them will never be able to have that sense of closure that they so desperately long for.

If you never experience pain you will never know the true joy of what it means to find happiness. Gratitude is a dish best served on a bed of humility. It makes for easier digestion. Success requires that triumph be recognized even in the midst of tragedy. It is all a part of the maturing process.

"U"

Understand Yourself Daily!

"Life isn't about finding yourself.
Life is about creating yourself."
—George Bernard Shaw

I can remember being 21 years old, and in my senior year of college at Clark Atlanta University. At that time, I knew I had an interest in working in the public sector. However, I was undecided whether or not I wanted to go in to politics, law enforcement, or the bureaucracy.

Looking back I think I have gone through or attempted at least 4 or 5 different professional paths. From local government, social work, law enforcement, music, business and now education, I have been able to investigate various fields by trying them on for size.

The one constant for me has been my love for and ability to relate to people. Now at the ripe age of 34 ☺ , I can honestly say that I have already lived about 3 different lives based upon the experiences I've had. In order to get the most out of life you must allow yourself the flexibility to change and grow.

I can honestly say that I do not have the same wants, wishes, fears or desires that I had at 21. Since then, I have developed new ones. God willing I will continue to do so. Each day that life gives is a chance for you to return the favor. Give life! As you live daily, identify those things that are important to you and grow them for the betterment of humanity. The world may not thank you for it, but you will be able to thank yourself. Always remember to check your personal inventory.

"V"

Vehemently Despise Evil!

*"Never open the door to the lesser evil; for other
and greater ones invariably slink in after it."*
—Baltasar Gracian

There are certain experiences that you do not have to have to know that they are not for you. Intelligent curiosity can sometimes be circumvented for prophetic insight. Contrary to what some may think, there is such a thing as evil. Now evil may not show itself like such infamous fictional Hollywood motion picture characters such as *Jason Voorhees, Freddie Kruger* or the *Candyman*. Evil is all around us. Evil may most likely reveal itself in the negative energy that may be exuded by the people who are around you. The type of energy that you allow to be a part of your space will begin to invade your space if you let them.

Do not waste your time on things and or people that do not have your best interest at heart. Positive qualities translate into positive experiences. You have a responsibility to position yourself to receive and give your best in everything you engage in. This is within your power and sphere of influence.

"W"

Wishing, Wanting
& Waiting . . .

"If your ship doesn't come in, swim out to it."
—Jonathan Winters

As human beings, we all have a wealth of desires and inner most thoughts. These desires could be for personal things such as health, wealth, employment or that "perfect" relationship. We spend a lot of time in self-reflection, thinking about a number of issues such as political affairs, family, finances, and other social concerns.

However, the spending of this "time" in stagnation could be considered an incubation period. Sometimes your level of desire will determine the extent of our actions you are willing to take when working towards a goal.

The first stage in this process is what I like to call "**wishing**." This process involves having a dream or vision of what you would like to accomplish. Because it is your dream, nothing is too far fetched. Too often, we sell ourselves short of ever accomplishing greatness because we don't allow ourselves to see the possibility of what we can imagine. No one has to see or believe in your dream but you. (At least not at the beginning . . .)

The second stage in this process is what I like to call "**wanting**." The *American Heritage Dictionary* defines the word want as: 1) The condition of lacking something usual or necessary; 2) A pressing need. When you become serious about reaching your goals, a shift within your countenance begins to take place. You will begin to focus more energy on things that you need more so than things that may only have had a mere "wish" or taste for. How bad do you want it? When you are able to answer this question with a profound sense of urgency, you know you have reached the place that you **want** to be.

The third stage in the process is what I like to call "**waiting**." The *American Heritage Dictionary* defines the word wait as: 1) to remain in expectation; 2) to be ready for use. In order to embrace waiting you must first divest yourself of those things that have negatively invested in you. (Be listening, hearing and receiving those things that matter.) Timing is the key to making the right decision. If you rush through expectation, you may miss your window of opportunity.

"X"

Extreme Situations Call for Grounded People!

"In extreme situations, the entire universe becomes our foe; at such critical times, unity of mind and technique is essential—do not let your heart waiver."
—Morihei Ueshiba

One of the most influential life lessons I learned came from one of my all-time favorite poems, *"IF"* by Rudyard Kipling. I memorized this poem in elementary school to participate in an oratorical contest. (I won of course!) The first line of the poem states, *"If you can keep your head when all about you are losing theirs and blaming it on you . . ."* Difficult situations require that you are able to navigate your way even in the midst of a storm.

One of my favorite television shows is *Unsung*. This cable show depicts current whereabouts of great artists of the past. In a recent episode, the featured artist was Evelyn "Champagne" King. In her prime, Evelyn was one of the most popular and powerful female artists around. During her life she faced a great deal of pain.

In watching her story unfold, it was revealed that she gave birth to a child that was born premature and had a number of physical challenges. Her miracle daughter lived for two years before she passed away. Had it not been for her family and her faith, Evelyn would not have made it through that experience.

As life continues to unfold, we must remember that we have a responsibility to continuously make adjustments. Trials and tribulations can eventually give birth to triumph. However, you cannot lose hope in faith or lose faith in hope. Never let anyone or anything get the best of you. You should give it freely!

"Y"

You Can't Win
If You're Not in the Game!

*"Life has no limitations except
the ones you make."*
—Les Brown

I like to consider myself to be an avid sports fan. I love all teams that are Miami: The "U", HEAT, Miami Dolphins, Marlins and yes even the FIU Golden Panthers (one of my Alma Maters) . . . If I'm not there in person, I'm watching them on television or listening on my satellite radio in the car.

Needless to say that it did pain me to watch two separate major sporting events recently and there were no Miami teams represented; The NFL AFC Wildcard Playoffs and the 2012 BCS National Championship Game.

Both of these events involved four great professional and collegiate football teams. The NFL AFC Playoff Game showcased the Denver Broncos vs. the Pittsburgh Steelers.

The BCS National Championship Game showcased the Alabama Crimson Tide vs. the LSU Tigers.

Now between the two games, I found the NFL Wildcard Playoff Game to be the most intriguing. The game was entertaining. I found it to be magical for one reason only, the "Tebow Factor". Tim Tebow in his fearless performance did what his critics said he would not and could not do. For all the doubters, his faith in God, belief in himself, and trust in his teammates gave him a blessed sense of determination. In overtime, on the first play from scrimmage, Tebow threw a touchdown pass to win the game. How is that for a storybook ending?

On the road of success, determination and desire meet at an intersection called destiny. If you are not willing to take ownership of your role as a member of "team life" you will never reach your destination.

"3"

Zeal Can Take You Where Knowledge Can't!

"Both trees and weeds grow from the ground up. Which one are you?"
—Jai A. Ingraham

Opportunities abound! The question is will you be ready for them when they come? Better yet how many opportunities can you create for yourself? Have you had any opportunities lately?

We are currently living in some of the most dismal economic times that we have ever experienced in this country and even throughout the world. However, it is still possible for you to be successful and to accomplish whatever it is that you are willing to <u>work</u> for.

For many people, zeal is the missing ingredient that keeps people from being able to take advantage of the best that life has to offer. Your zeal for positive energy can actually demand to only receive positive energy from others. Having enthusiasm, humble confidence, and being adaptable can make all the difference in the world. No one person was born with all the answers. Nevertheless, exuding the right attitude with zeal and gusto can get you a seat at the table. In the dinning room of life that's all one can hope for. Now, what you do after you get in your seat is up to you. Remember, you have the power to make others want to experience more of you!

A Call to Action

Now is the time for you to step into the realization of your destiny! A sense of purposeful urgency should guide the decisions as you make moving forward. Failure, faith, trials and triumph will all meet you on your journey to a destination of success. You must be willing to **will** yourself. Be relentless in your pursuit to be your best and to share your best with others. You have the potential to become more powerful than you could ever imagine. My telling is nothing in comparison to your believing.

Final Thoughts

As I have come to the close of this my first book, I want to leave you with a care package to take with you on your road to total success. Many believe that the number 13 is an unlucky number. In the words of the legendary Hip Hop group Public Enemy, *"Don't believe the hype!"* Your perception and perspective can make all the difference. The following is a list of 13 powerful statements that I have created to give you inspiration for your journey. You should read and repeat this list 13 times daily until it becomes a part of your countenance.

WORDS TO LIVE BY:

1. **BETWEEN VOCATION & VACATION LIES VISION. FIND YOUR OWN!**

2. **EMBRACE THE YOU THAT YOU WANT TO BECOME!**

3. **YOUR DESTINY WILL ONLY TAKE YOU WHERE YOU DIRECT IT!**

4. **SUCCESS CAN ONLY HAPPEN WHEN FEAR IS CONQUERED BY FAITH AND BECOMES FAVOR!**

5. **POWER IS ONLY POTENT WHEN IT IS FUELED BY PASSION!**

6. **IF YOU SHAKE SOMEONE'S HAND, THEY CAN'T PUSH YOU DOWN. THEY CAN ONLY PULL YOU IN THE DIRECTION YOU LET THEM!**

7. **TRUST IN GOD, BELIVE IN YOURSELF, AND HAVE FAITH IN OTHERS!**

8. **YOU ALREADY HAVE EVERYTHING YOU NEED TO BE GREAT!**

9. **IN ORDER TO GET SOMETHING THAT YOU'VE NEVER HAD, YOU MUST BE WILLING TO DO SOMETHING THAT YOU'VE NEVER DONE!**

10. **FEAR IS ONLY AS POWERFUL AS YOUR LACK OF FAITH!**

11. **OTHERS' EXPECTATIONS CAN BECOME YOUR LIMITATIONS IF YOU LET THEM!**

12. **LET THE LIFE YOU WANT BECOME THE LIFE YOU LIVE!**

13. **THERE IS POWER IN YOUR POTENTIAL AND PROVISION FOR YOUR PROMISE!!!**

Lastly, there is one final gift that I wish to leave with you. God has blessed me with several gifts. Poetry is one of them. Since it is known that you never get a second chance to make a first impression, I am going to make sure that this last impression is the first thing that comes to mind when you think of this work. If this poem were a child, I would liken it to my firstborn! Let these words resound within your soul and propel you to great success. You are worth it!!!

"The Power Within You"

The power within you,
Is greater than what the world can see;
Untapped is your potential,
You control your destiny.

Engage every situation,
As a chance to test your wit;
Although you may be met with resistance,
Never let your spirit quit!

Trust your instincts,
And have faith in yourself;
Your experience has value,
Always look within, if no place else.

Focus on your mission,
Keep your message clear;
Others may not see your vision,
Until you make it appear.

When it is all said and done,
And there is nothing more that you can do;
Have peace knowing you gave your best,
Remember, the power lies within you!

Copyright © 2010 Jai A. Ingraham

About The Author

Jai A. Ingraham, the "Inspirational Motivator" is an educator, entrepreneur, speaker, author, poet, lecturer and vocalist. Known for blending a passion for inspiring others with his love for music, his high energy messages strike cords with the young and old alike. As a member of the African Methodist Episcopal Church, Jai has a strong foundation in Christian Leadership and Ministry. He is a highly sought after motivator, workshop presenter and keynote speaker for religious based organizations, non-for-profit entities and educational institutions. His life-long goal is to Educate, Motivate and Inspire all who he encounters.

Professionally, Jai has a varied and diverse background. He has worked in private industry, municipal government, non-for-profit agencies, K-12 education, and higher education. Currently he is an Assistant Principal with Miami-Dade County Public Schools and an Instructor of Cultural Diversity with the University of Phoenix, respectively. He serves as a member of the Board of Directors for the Fatherhood Task Force of South Florida, Inc. and the Center for Family and Child Enrichment, Inc. Jai is a State of Florida Notary Public and is the President and Chief Executive Officer of I-Inspire, Inc.

Jai holds a Bachelor of Arts degree in Political Science from Clark Atlanta University, a Master of Public Administration from Florida International University, and a Graduate Certificate in Educational Administration from St. Thomas University. He is currently pursuing a Doctor of Education degree from Northeastern University. Jai and his wife Karen reside in Miami Gardens, Florida with their two daughters Kiara and Jaicey. Learn more about Jai at *www.jaispeaks.com*.

Stay connected with Jai on Social Media:
Facebook
Linkedin
YouTube
Twitter